Pure
Filth

Pure
Filth

Aidan Mathews

THE LILLIPUT PRESS
DUBLIN

First published 2023 by
THE LILLIPUT PRESS
62–63 Sitric Road, Arbour Hill
Dublin 7, Ireland
www.lilliputpress.ie

Various poems have previously appeared in the *Irish Times*, RTÉ,
Southword, *The Spectator*, *The Tablet* and *Temenos*.

ISBN 9781843518754

A CIP record for this title is available
from The British Library.

1 3 5 7 9 10 8 6 4 2

Set in 11.5 pt on 18 pt Quixote by iota (iota-books.ie)
Printed in Spain by Graphycems

For Iseult, Vanessa, and Eloise:
three tambourines in the labyrinth

Contents

9

POINTER FOR USER INTERFACE

In the same way that my intimate emails
Arrive in my wife's warm I-Phone pinging
With a semi-state disclaimer in the first official language,
These too, the Metamorphoses of Covid,
Come with a caveat in my forked mother-tongue:
Old English, Middle French, Aramaic-American.

This poetry is full of flashing imagery.
It was coded in a year of imperfect vision
And may already be outdated or give scandal.
Its cursor blinks at nobody under forty,
Preferably biblical, years, since its only helpline
Is the helpless frontline of the line that follows it

On its own two feet – hendecasyllables, sort of –
To where the reader's lost each one of their longings
And belongs now to their losses. That is plenitude.
There's no excuse, of course, for the editorial –
Greek to us all, the gibberish of empire –
That the Occident is not itself an accident,

Except to plead that this paleface, being exposed
As a neonate to the eastern Mediterranean,

Spent sorrowful decades on her psycho-active scriptures
And the addictive sedative formerly called Quintilian.
Block this incendiary sender, so, all his alms and amn'ts.
Filter such filth going forward. Report all spam.

I

*The highest duty of the lover is to stand
guard over the solitude of the loved one.*

—Rilke

RHAPSODY IN PINK

for Iseult

In the Rotunda delivery suite
Muffled midsummer sounds
Seep through an eighteenth-century sash.

Your clarinet solo a police siren,
That ambulance horn a baritone sax,
The traffic's tympani and trombones

With jackhammers, wrecking balls,
And the street-painter's Christ
Of a pro-life procession.

A Roma there on cardboard, a barber
Chorus, a barefoot clubber
Clutching her heels, and a vixen

From the Garden of Remembrance
Cat-walking the tramlines
En route from Chinatown

To a bin in Little Africa.
This is for you, a daughter's daughter,

My own, my amniotic city

As the midwives wash you briskly
Within sight of a freshwater faucet
Where I'd meet my own granddad,

Gabardine open, tie thrown back,
And humming good old Gershwin
At the marble tub of the font.

He remembered drinking from it
Like a street-corner baptistery
Among draft-horses twenty hands high

Where you come gushing now, brand-new,
With a widow's peak and wizened feet
And seeing the world in sepia.

BOW FOR A BRIGID'S CROSS

Sleet on the gravel could be salt-grit
Or it may be confetti.
Then the soft weather lifts,
Smiles through her fretting
Tears like a Chekhov coquette:
All corsage now and no corsetry.
This is it, then. The groundswell,
Lá Fhéile Bríde, greenery
Stealing her march on Britain,
Healing a whole month's mind,
Breathing on window-boxes.

A note on our wet boot-scraper
Lists laundry and ironing done.
It's from Rainbow, a Zambian.
She has shut the gate behind her
As quietly as flannel, and moved on;
While the girl in the bedsit opposite
Models a retro gypsy skirt
At her vanity slimming mirror.
Such primrose and violet tints!

Like the pastel espadrilles

Of my bride of forty Februaries
Who's singing down in the dinette
The refrain on her mobile Spotify
Of a hit from the last millennium –
Our album, its attic vinyl
A surface scratched by styluses –
As she fastens a hook-on high chair
For the child of a child of a child
At her maiden Candlemas.

FALLING IN

Your mother began with the bum shuffle.
You have chosen instead the commando crawl
Across the no man's land of hall and lounge
Through circuit-boards, computer cables, all
The entanglements of table-legs, to sprawl there,

Face to the floor. Thus my great-grand uncle
Whose Mass I served on the jubilee of the Somme.
His brass cross made from soldered bullet casings
And perched now on a plinth of shrapnel shell
Was brought in starlight to the dying conscripts.

They were not crying for fathers. Phantom flares
Whitewashed the legless and the disembowelled
Who had called only for *Mutti, Matka, Mam,*
The password of the speechless, of the spooked child
Wobbling, and toddling, and then falling in.

A BIRTHING STOOL
for Laura

When you were sleepless in your Moses basket,
I was basket-weaving down in the O.T. glasshouse
Night terrors on memory foam in the hospital.

When you stood on your own two feet in a bandstand,
It was no walk in the park for you or your mother.
I said to the daffodils: *Don't.* To the bluebells: *Why?*

I this. I that. I, the other: a farewell to welfare
Like the thirty-one chapter headings of *Robinson Crusoe*.
I had smiles to go before I wept, and I beamed broadly

A prayer not to be preyed upon. I thought in italics:
Let my shadow be her shade so in the ultraviolet light
Somehow, Thou Ghost of a God, from lambing to shambles.

That was the blur of the second millennium. This is 20/20.
Your baby, the double of you, is smiling here in a bassinet
With the smell of a fresh pastel, a whiff of Aloe Vera.

The child's stool that you sat on can stay there, out in
   the shed,

With the post-war Underwood keyboard, a portable
 Golf Ball.
There will be sand-tables, paddle-pools, and no
 ant-powder.

A tricycle bell will chime to mark thirty-three years.
Then a toddler will climb up the slide in the butterfly
 playground
And down the rungs of the ladder in a slow reversal

Towards hands that are splayed, no longer shaking
 with tablets,
Unfolded and *orans* now, as she springs from the shock-
 absorbent
Cinders under my feet to sweep me off them.

HOUSEKEEPER

In your enormous dormer room
Forty carpet-rods from the letterbox,
A flight over the nursery,
I saved the front pages of burning issues.

Kennedy Shot. Two Men Land On the Moon,
Thirteen Dead in the Bogside. Saigon Falls.
You said they'd be valuable someday.
They're not worth the paper they're written on.

Now I think of you rolling yesterday's
Property Supplement in the fire-place
Of the big study, of the cold drawing-room
And the little grate where you taught me the *Hail Mary*.

Such expertise in the sleek twist
Of the steam-burned hand, in the low
Breathing on the smoke of newsprint
And a damp acorn from the nuns' cemetery.

This morning's edition on the window sill
Is already the jaundice of Yellow Journals.
There are more life-rafts off Lampedusa,

Stick-women trekking North to find West,

And charity texts you can tap for three euro
To Sight Savers and to Save the Children.
I'd stretch, if I could, to the highest brass handle
In the wormwood tallboy where I stored Biafra

And even the bombing of Nelson's Pillar,
To the sock drawer's small side-panel
Where you tuck the pocket insurance book
To cover the costs of your funeral.

LAUREL FOR A LADY

after Petrarch

She who was Ann has now become another
Whose real absence is more present still.
Hers was a summer solstice, four full seasons,
Something that scintillated; something stellar ...

The star-child shines again, there in the wash-house,
Merry and private while I crank the mangle.
It's she herself: she is as was, yet will be.
Say *amn't* to me, pet. Say: *I do be tired, love.*

Sometimes she blows balloons; sometimes says nothing.
I wake for Maalox. There's no hint of halogen.
The galaxies are closer than her mouth ulcers.

A hospice clock tut-tutted. Then she vanished.
It was the Feast of the Lord's Transfiguration
As the peace-bell in Hiroshima pealed a dawn chorus.

KEENING CILLIAN

i.m Cillín de Bhaldraithe, late of Coillte

What shall we do without the wry woodsman?
Cut down like a cash-crop conifer
For a Christmas tree, for a nest of tables,
The trestle of a bench in a beer garden
Or a carving board for the ogham of knives.

He was forty-seven. He was a father,
The spit of his own dad. Fire at the funeral
Fed on his casket. Pining, a wife watched
Poplar or willow wade through the furnace:
An oaken dugout, a long-ship flaring.

No birdsong now in the state plantation
But the Polish women grubbing for mushrooms.
Your midlife finds you in a darker forest
Where you can't tell the wood from the trees,
Hazel from rowan, native from alien.

I wish you branches. I wish you broadleaves.
May you scale and abseil like a pine-marten,
Agile, all flight and no landfall,
From the London plane trees in the Pale of Dublin

With its dead Dutch elms, its pollarded limes,

To Connemara alders and the bog myrtle
That is called *raideog* in De Bhaldraithe's Dictionary.
May your seedling child, a sapling staked now
With wire and rubber like a polio caliper,
Spill open in time an April canopy

For shrews with their trumpet ears, for trekkers,
For the anguish of foxes mating in the roots,
And entrust the true North of quicksilver lichen
To the helicopter keys of her own fruiting:
Daughter to father, green ash to white ashes.

STEPWELLS

A two-year-old tiptoes on hot Kerry sand
Across a strand that is luminous at night
With the stencil of a starfish in her fist.

This will sleep on in my hippocampus,
A spike-strip at an abandoned border-post,
Until it dawns again in the soft scrunch

Of the barefoot, fake-tanned tippy toes
On gravel at the gate, her high heels off
After the drunken dance-floor, after the Debs.

The child pulls at my ponytail like a harness.
I lift her onto my shoulders to see the Atlantic,
White of my wave, weight of my world. Us.

This too turns in its sleep without waking
As a creeper glosses barbed perimeter wire
And the moth cocoons, a ball of wax in the eardrum.

Then there's a Snapchat shot of her perched
High on her boyfriend's back at the sub-bass speakers,
Mouthing a chart hit I've never heard of.

There was even a line across the estuary,
Netting to stop the nudists, mines in the water.
Now it is crystal clear. Now it is in my depth.

On my day-release, she'd wait at the window
With the bear who talked and who read her stories
Nobody saw on the spotless vellum. Say it.

Like today, the first thing this morning,
She stood in her mask at the passion-flower vine
Between the green bin and the double buggy

In the metamorphoses of Covid Y2,
And raised her toddler to the glass I kiss
And mist, and clear, and kiss, but cannot open.

MAYDAY
for Lucy and Ronan

On a wedding day that was to have been
We walk in the grounds of the school that grew me.
Grey squirrels in the practice nets, still bluebells

Where there were bluebells in the last millennium;
And the best of the cherry blossom briefly
A grubby confetti no parish permitted.

I am not walking you up a flowered church aisle
But a lane of linden and a boundary hedge
With last year's leaves rusted among green shoots.

Marcescent, said the priest who taught us trees
And roamed their roots to gather his May altar,
Just as we're now processing at two metres.

And this is not a toast by the bride's father
With all its pauses and its punchlines marked.
It is a word of warming and a wish-you-well.

Your bridal white's become the grey of scrubs,
The dress a gown and boots, the veil a visor,

Both meals postponed, the Mass and marquee gone.

This is your quarantine, your forty days;
The first of summer always an emergency
And an emergence, love. These are forever married.

TREADING WATER
For my deep-water grand-daughter-in-waiting

On the day of your four-month scan
The boats set out for the Dunkirk beaches:
Paddle-steamers, pedalos, ketches,
A spinnaker eighty years on.

The anomaly test
Came after the Normandy knees-up,
The veterans' wheelchairs on the platform
Leaving tricycle tracks in the sand.

Since then, it's been normal mostly:
Mainly children in shorts and T-shirts,
Stone-still and whiffy in the ebb-tide rock-pools,
Curled up in the foetus,

Their mothers floating face-down
In the same charcoal scarf my mother wore
Among *tondues* on the esplanade at Menton,
One miscarriage after the Second World War.

Their bellies bloat like the fullness of time
And the gulls love them. They go straight for the lips.

They gorge on the open eyes like oysters
And the sea salivates.

But you, you are still there treading water,
Alive and almost kicking last Tuesday at two;
Nameless, stateless, paperless, pale,
A refugee under the Dublin Agreement,

And of less consequence to the court, my Lord,
Than an otter's kitten on the Dodder river
Or the eighteen protected species of moss
In an unmarked convent orphanage plot.

Avoid all boardwalks and breakwaters.
Say nothing at customs. Declare only yourself.
Raise your arms in the harsh helium light
And cry out in the Esperanto of pain.

Risk the soft inflatable womb of the world,
Precarity of its patched rubber rafting.
In the Fertile Crescent of a new moon's curve,
Drift into the cove of this, your christening.

SIGNS

Still tell us *Welcome to the Gaeltacht*
In the old uncial of the Celtic script
My school abandoned with the Roman collar
In the decade after the Kennedy visit
When his half-dollar was legal tender
For cap-gun ammo at an Irish college.

Bienvenue, *Willkommen* too.
An End of Rainbow poster flags it:
The combined Am Drams' legendary
Chamber of Commerce *Cabaret*
At the Holy Family parish hall
In aid of the borstal's overhaul.

We drive among sale-agreed ruins
Where the signal fails on Spotify
And the wind frowns on a graphite lake.
It whines in the Moses' baskets
Of the bog-cotton and moor-grass
And it passes over the private beats

My father fished from. In the rear-view mirror
That mirror writing of *slliK ssenderiT*

Must be *Tiredness Kills* or *Something Tuirse*.
No sight of quad bikes, Pampas grass,
The convex lens at cattle-grid gateways
Or a boy as big as his dad's thigh-wader.

I look back over the Honda's head-rest
To a child in the front of a Chevrolet
Who has pencilled a postcard to his nanny
In his Montessori Hiberno-English:
I am in Ireland on holiday, Nurse.
Please get the Valiant *early on Thursday.*

And the postcard morphs to a mobile phone
That can pick up nothing. *'Are we there yet?'*
Moans a grand-child strapped like a moon-lander.
Until we're in range of the refugee bivouac
In the failed Fáilte motel that was twinned
With a town in Texas, the clue is *ciúnas*.

A MAP OF IRELAND

On the other side of the wallpaper
My father's finished his night prayer.
The timbers creak, a clinker-built boat.
He is battening bay windows.

His antacid froths in tap-water.
The clink of the egg spoon stirring it
Is the tinkle of wire shrouds and halyards,
His gulp the slosh of a hull's gurgle.

Car-lights like the oars of currachs
Sweep and scull the ceiling in silence.
The hood of my angle-poise has cooled
In the foghorn's sperm-whale sonar.

And the gecko in my groin
Bristles on my stomach like a lizard,
A bearded dragon iguana
To be petted into a Prince Charming.

I hang my miraculous medal
On the stanchion of the head-board
And drift like a floating kelp-forest

To a far, forbidden Galapagos.

On the other side of the bulkhead
My birth mother is snoring softly.
Her turquoise candlewick coverlet
Lolls and lifts, a lilo, a life-raft,

While my father dreams of sailing
Around the globe on his own cutter,
His hold stowed with Irish potatoes
Like old Sir Francis Chichester.

In his sickbay across the landing
My dying brother weighs
The sour breeze from the estuary,
Odour of menses and morgue.

He will moor in the cove of no calm.
His mermaids will be manatees only.
They will make few waves in the sea-wash
For a knight unharnessed by white horses.

And the housekeeper there in her lazarette,
Child of none and mother of many,
Will be swept off her feet by the ocean's *Aves*

In the white exile of her own body.

This, then, is the log of those small hours,
Landfall of moonlight, honour guard of gull,
Lee of my counter-tenor's shearwater,
All coastlines a cloud-shape calving.

It is half a hundred years now, and not fifty;
A salt-flat of faint watermarks left
Where my sperm once smelled like a storm of tears,
My tears a slipstream of semen.

IN PASSING

All that my daughter will remember of him –
The surgeon under searchlights, the sailor beating upwind,
The father who shook hands with his five sons each
    meeting –
Is the stock-still figure standing in the yacht-club
    dining-room
Who drools saliva on his fawn loafers.

Which is where he told me once that his only image
Of the granny who lived on the ground-floor of his home
Is the sash-cord tearing and the box bay window frame
Suddenly chuting to crush her knuckles and kill her
Before the bumble-bee had blundered its way out.

The terraces dry and the vine-trees cannot weep for them.
The cellars sink like sediment. Maybe a wine-cork bobs
Like the deckchair carried ashore by the last Blasket
    islander –
Among oars that had been rafters and rafters that were
    hoarded –
With the Latin word for Portugal inscribed on its head-rest.

RÉPARATION

Incisors bloody from flossing
Under hard overhead light,
He spots her make-up in the mirror
For the first time since that night:
Her foundation, her concealer.

Each bottle-neck upside down
And shelved according to depth
Like a water glass arpeggio,
A flight of steps that are left
On the ledge at the frosted window.

He assumes her yoga pose,
The half-moon, to read them right:
Labels on empty cosmetic
Flasks and phials of a life
Beyond laxatives, Nicorette patches.

There's serum and balm and *Restore*,
Revitalize, Ultra-Brite,
Age Perfect Golden Age,
And the duty-free eyeliner
From the fishnet bag at the terminal.

He scents her moisturizer,
The fake-tanned throat and tendons,
A target cross in her cleavage
From the age of the backless dress,
The stage of the ghost bikini.

And he bows down to the sinkhole,
His mouth a zero of pan stick
From the smears of scrolled-up Colgate
As his chalk lips open to gargle,
Then gag, on mouthwash from Lidl.

SEARCH HISTORY

It's Sunday, late. Lights out, stars on; the moon
Waxed lyrical. He would have said that to her.
Is it the green bin then or is it the black bin?

The wheelie thing would be out the gate already
In the time it took her to have staple-gunned
The seam of his chino-pocket or to have squirted
Olive detergent in the water nozzle
Of the Audi's wipers for the street's tree-resin,
Its slow sepia sap on the blurred windshield.

She would have said: *The mind boggles.*
You and your Googling. You and your Wikipedia.

He smokes there in the porch as if she were safe inside
Cleaning the coasters with a chamois after a night-cap.
The tiles still smell of cologne like a private chapel
From the atomiser that she shattered there
On the last shop of all. At Till Number Three.
The disabled bag-filler blinked, breathing
Salt-and-vinegar shock through her poor public teeth
At the same cerebral tremble in the left-handed lady.

He is not yet fifty. He is half a hundred.
There are so many answers left to be questioned, yet
He knows the churches only by their street-names
And the night-sky pales at the thought of a star-chamber.

She would have said: *The mind boggles.*
You and your Googling. You and your Wikipedia.

Now his enormous portal
Lifts like the apse of that basilica,
A dome somewhere in Africa – somewhere in his Search
    History –
Where clouds condense under the oculus
To smatter the empty sanctuary with an indoor drizzle
And the swifts that summer in red-brick Dublin
Practise their fluent flight-paths. They do not mate,
As myth imagines, in their freefall; but for life,
In a mid-air monogamy.

She would have said: *The mind boggles.*
You and your Googling. You and your Wikipedia.

UNCLE JACK

A century after, your gene-pool stirs no ripple.
Were you aged three when you died or a toddler still?
Had you the Mathews jowl or the McHenry nostril?
And why do we always call it the Spanish Flu

When it happened here in Donnybrook, South Dublin,
Where you will never become the rogue grand-uncle
With the labrador smell of waistcoat and pipe-smoke
For my children jumping on your crochet cushions.

We were told the cert says *atypical pneumonia*
In much the way that the census, eight years earlier,
Made a travelling salesman of a great grandfather
Who worked through the Famine as a night dung-carter.

All I know is that your wooden train carriage
Of a whole hundred Easters since this foolish April
Rose that same Christmas as my father's fire-engine
With new rungs painted like a barber's pole

On a ladder all blood and bandages. Outside,
There was holly once and not crepe on the door-knocker.
Still the smiling, senile granny who would watch

Soldiers in skullcaps pray at the Western Wall

And hear talk of a moon-shot – *Is that actual fact now?* –
Wore black through the Paris Maypole and the Prague
    Spring
For the atrocity of a transient she had borne with
In the war of the three cousins who began it as kings.

NOTICES

My birth was fan-fared in the Saturday *Irish Times*
With a flight of listed siblings, a *Deo Gratias,*
The fountain-pen entry in the family Bible
And christening cufflinks for my First Communion Mass.

Your cabbage-leaf arrival in the *Evening Herald*
Mumbles: *A healthy and attractive baby girl*
From a good family background. C/O:
Catholic Protection and Rescue, Reverend Chaplain.

As I'm handed back at the font to an orphanage nurse
By a Great War veteran, a padre hardened to Canon,
Your teenage mother will top and tail you in well-water
For a curate to bundle into the back-seat of an Anglia;

Which, as it happened, was the exact same model
My father bought for my mother because she had borne
A seventh child, a crier, and would be worn to the bone
Save for those silver pedals that took the weight off her soles.

Imagine, my wife says, *if mine went to work in Dagenham,*
Who would stuff bears with a pedal pump in a
      Wolverhampton plant;

And the plot thickens: her Sligo headstone's shadowed
By somebody's huge cenotaph, who died in the Twin
    Towers.

DOG DAYS

The mother of my children
Leaks as she laughs.
At her online Pilates
The futon is waterproof.

In Lidl, I'm looking for
Antacids, panty-liners,
Who once asked for lubricants
In an Istanbul chemist.

Only the algorithms
Of a YouTube search engine
Could guess what I'm fretting for
As I post off my poo

For a lucky dip Bowel Screen.
First the implants, then the transplant.
My stretch-marked stomach,
Like the *linea negra*

Of her last trimesters
Grandchildren ago,
Secretes her spare kidney.
It is meds now at bedtime

As we pile up the pillows.
The panic button's toggle
Glows a night-light in tinfoil.
That webcam at our gable-end

Will eavesdrop in sepia
On a lamp-lit debutante
Or a new neighbour's hybrid
Looted for its lithium,

While we spoon in the duvet,
Who feasted, knife and fork,
When the canteen we first shared
Was a rucksack's turquoise hipflask.

On the Neighbourhood WhatsApp –
Among handymen's mobiles,
Emojis of tears, updates
On hooded louts at the Luas –

Let the missed calls accumulate.
I do my press-ups in the Downward Dog.
Herself, in the calm of the Corpse pose,
Laughs again till she leaks.

THE OLD DEAR

Darling, let's leave this world the way we started
With the private pet-names of our wedding night
Before my crow's feet and your stretch-marked stomach.

I may be older than Methusaleh
And you yourself, well, close to a certain age:
You're still my sweetheart, I'm your bestest boy.

What more do we need to know of this last throw
Except that our Fall has been a bumper harvest
With notes of Bordeaux cedar in its nose.

From the Latin of Ausonius of Aquitaine (390 AD)

MARLBORO MAN

You were there at my side when I lost my virginity.
You were there, joined at the hip, when I found it again.

Through the years of night-terrors on memory foam,
Of change for the payphone in the closed ward,

And in the basilica on the lake among the barefoot
And the monastery on Mount Athos for the Easter Vigil;

Along the yellow-brick road of the El Camino Real,
As a post-grad High Plains drifter in Palo Alto,

Writing poems about the peripheries from the centre
    of power
While the Mexican wetbacks rolled out lawn from a
    trailer truck;

In the Tenderloin streets with the X's and no Franciscan,
On the island paths to the temples one cigarette distant;

At the shape-shifts of her belly like a sand-dune, drifting;
At the Moses crib in the corner, at my AWOL stool-
    weaving;

With a daughter, the pee and nicotine of our walkabout,
Who would suck my cigarette finger like an inhaler

As I lay in a lithium pool of the salt Dead Sea
Where the hills are levelled and the valleys are filled in;

And on 9/11, when I sat on the edge of my bed at the
     plasma set
With my unwashed feet in a moon of talcum powder.

Until today, after rainfall, the sky smiling through its
     tears,
Amidst a meteor shower of my own floaters,

I can see on the MRI a murmuration of shades
That have risen up, fuming, from the grey waste of my
     seashell ashtray

To leave me open-mouthed at last, to leave me breathless,
My worry-beads, my rosary, my jailer's clutch of house-
     keys,

My morning prayer, companion of the small hours,
Ashram of the angle-poise, of the wry pause and the line-
     break.

As smoke is driven away, Psalm something, so am I driven.
Now I do for you as you will do for me. I scatter your ashes.

IN PRAISE OF OLDER MEN

The last time I stripped in front of a woman,
She was a skin specialist. Mine crawled on all fours.

A Mayfair girl-next-door, a beer-garden and bum,
Jutting her lip to lift the blonde fringe of her highlights.

But they'd be my age now, the flames of the two-bar fire
    in a bedsit,
Mandy of Paddington Station and the mail-boat back

At breakfast television in her stair-lift chalet.
Yet this melanin yummy mummy from the Mayo Clinic

Left me my Y-Fronts and miraculous medal. I stood there,
My hands at my holster sides like a cowboy shootout.

It was all the twenty-third psalm and the twenty-third
    chromosome,
Same as the girl with the star tattoo in Greek Street

The year the Cinzano light went out in Piccadilly
When what started at Stratford closed in an Angus
    Steakhouse.

All I wanted was this one to look at my forehead, my face;
The Cupid's bow of my muzzle, the new, flossed caps.

History has not been kind to the heritage site of my body
But even a ruin can edify. For Jesus' sake, look,

I made love with a Latin hippy on the Hill of the Nymphs
     in Athens
When the news came through that De Valera had died.

But that was the era of Ambré Solaire and the sleek oil of
     its slapstick,
And this is my future of Factor Fifty. This is trilby time, lad.

She touches the stain on my cheek like the bishop at
     Confirmation.
I hear what she mouths. My ears lengthen like Africa.

We are dating now, us two. Same day six months,
     God willing,
Smart in those Puma boxers the sons-in-law wear.

DOORS OPENING, DOORS CLOSING

I soar to the third floor of a hospital
In a mirrored lift like a three-leaf dressing table
To a glacier of white walls, white ceiling lights, white
    sheets,
The snow-glare of a ward like Newfoundland.

I am being prepped, old friend. You are for post-mortem.
A name-tag on my wrist, a name-tag on your toe.
They are close-shaving my pubis. You will be embalmed.
The same chaplain will bring us Extreme Unction,

Two lots of loved ones pay the same parking toll,
And the same soprano voice in the elevator
Will tell us all: Doors opening, doors closing.
A century back, when we were undergraduates,

Full of paradox and the pleasures of oxymoron,
We'd have pulled some pretty girl out of the Arts Block
In a gypsy skirt, drop earrings, and a pair of espadrilles
With our dialectical flirting.

A packet of ten Major cost thirteen new pence,
And Time Now Please called for a round of lager.

If the hip chick slid her tongue into your mouth,
You could tease her muslin breast with your cigarette
   finger.

Now, late by several years for my own funeral,
I'm waiting here in a gown for my wife's kidney
And the stitch-in-time of a smiling seamstress surgeon.
The only sense you'll find is in symmetry,

You'd say, *not in the sign of the question mark*
But the figure eight cut into meltwater
Like a double negative that dissolves zero.
I hold the morphine pump like a child's snow-globe

And the voice in the concrete shaft says: Doors opening,
Doors closing. Stand well back.
In a ward, one floor above my little ascension,
They are stripping your parts like a saint's relics.

There's a new cornea for a roofless temple
Of the Holy Ghost in Mullingar, maybe,
Another for a roadside shrine in Ballinasloe;
Heart, lungs, and a teetotaller's liver

By helicopter and motorbike courier

To those who are neither Jew nor Gentile,
Neither you nor me. They are sheathed in ice-packs
And not in amethyst or in ivory caskets

While the ransacked body in the lift going down,
Wrapped in white linen on a hostess trolley,
Unsettles the two young thirtysomethings
With my I-phone charger and Dairy Milk chocolates

Who are waiting to rise from the basement floor
To a patient whose chest wears a port like a bull's eye.
He has taken off both of his black Bose earbuds
To hear those accordion curtains fold and unfold.

II

Belief in a system is a failure in loyalty.

—Camus

REQUEST FOR A PROTEST POEM

No drums when it's done, though.
First, I delete the drafts;
Delete the deletions then.
In the aftermath of that,

Any and all A4
Backwards to where it started,
Each sheet in the shredder
Tickertape to no march

Through town but a standstill
So sudden we can't be sure
A procession paraded past
Between the brass and the roar.

Ditch handwritten notes as well,
Doodle and memo and post-it,
All leaf-litter for poop-scoops
When klaxon and bullhorn blare;

Leaving only the gift of itself
And the grind of it washed away
Like the wet glint of the cobbles
Hosed down after a demo.

ANNE FRANKED

They're down at the door again. It's the next set starting.
That jackboot step on the stair is the party snare-drum.
But I blow on the cuttlefish ink as it freezes,
So nothing is blotted; the margin white as a sheet.

In fact, I was selected from the get-go.
Now another file's being slipped in the starred folder.
The poster girl for a thousand and one pogroms –
Her DVD in the convent Montessori,

Lite-Ghetto Lit for the blonde book-clubbers
On a gated community's barbecue terrace –
Is trafficked, whisked out of Amsterdam
Where the windowed nudes are sitting like cellists

To a booth in a Feminist Studies fair-ground.
Yet I squat here still over a hand-mirror
From my great-grandmother's dance-card days,
My desk a bucket in a waterless closet;

And I part the pleats of myself to wonder.
How can a man get in through there?
Or a baby her streaming head around it?

Dear Daddy Pim will redact that, bless him,

For the Pan paperback with its photo-shopped poppet.
Such duty of care, his careful erasures!
I am red-lined where I should be red-lipped,
Washed white in a black-out, a spray-paint silhouette,

A spot-lit stencil, a see-though stage flat.
Frankly, I'm Anne. No atrocity pathos:
I was who I was from foundry to furnace.
Wish me Dutch courage, will you, in the true netherworld?

Listen out for my low, last *l'esprit d'escalier*
As I close my diary's cover to be worked through,
Collectable now, a corpus, with a genteel detective
Lightly linking my wrist for the last jitterbug.

LOCKDOWN NO LOCK-UP

How does a man self-isolate
Who has done so since his earliest childhood?
He is elated, naked, as he cartwheels now,
A tumble-turn through the red deserted neighbourhood,
Head over heels in love with the cleared city.

This is his perfect freedom for the first time.
Lying down like a crucifix on a motorway with no traffic
Or walking on stone back-walls the length of a period
    terrace
To watch the figures of eight, again and again, that an ant
Describes all morning on a single sandstone fossil.

In this, the ultimate asylum, all houses safe,
His emptiness escorts him through the wide streets.
Now it is his turn, it is his hard-earned right
To wave to the women and children at the locked windows
Who do not wave back, who are petrified statues now,

Immobilised by their medicine, its white bird-shit
Smeared on their lips and jawline, the stupid shuffling
    of soles.
In fact, he has never been better. He is free at last

In the closed wards of a locked-down Dublin suburb.

He has all the keys. Doors open. Now, at last, he is sealed.

HIBERNIAN CLEANING SERVICES

I wash my hands of newsprint and numbers
In the no-touch stream of the warm-air dryer
Where the toilet checklist is taped to the tiles.

All the gargled ogres from the Brothers Grimm –
Marek, Tadeusz, Karol, Igor –
Return to me now in my grinning brethren

From the stakes and the spikes of Middle Europe
As the smiling janitors of our office john;
And the black babies who've grown to be women –

Charity, Mercy, Maryam, Hope –
Have quit their rigid, rectangular countries
To make my bog-land smell like a pine forest.

The mirror mirrors mist. The furtive
Cistern hisses, faucets foam at the mouth,
And even the *ad hoc* smoking-room I've found

In the torture chamber of the invalid cubicle
Roars through the sonar of its plumbing
That weird waterfall music of the rock-ledged

Foothold hidden behind the cataract
Where fugitives hunkered in the old Hammer Horrors
From the witch-finders, from the searching torches,

The garrison dragging the rivers like hair,
And the unleashed, lunging vigilantes
Sinking their halberds into the haystacks.

To stand such ground is total immersion,
A freshet sprung from a granite recess
Like a struck stone, like an aquifer. And here comes Tina,

All Rubbermaid mop-head and aluminum bucket,
To sign on now with a lemon flow-pen
In Day-Glo capitals that are steam-and-waterproof.

CANCEL CULTURE

It's on Page One of my selected Dryden:
Heroic Stanzas Consecrated to
The Memory of His Highness Oliver,
Late Lord Protector of this Commonwealth.
ABAB, in stealthy pentameter,
The long and the short of it.

Skip to the verso of his *Astraea Redux*:
A Poem on the Happy Restoration
And Return of His Sacred Majesty Charles II.
It has taken Cinna less than three trimesters
To roll those rhyming couplets in the very same metre,
Drumbeat of Tweedledum and Tweedledee.

The bookmark between them is an An Lár bus-ticket
With pink font that prints out: *Táille, One Denarius.*
That's my father-in-law coming from work in Clery's
As the Roman blinds are lowered while the mannequins
    are dressed,
With his pocket-size dust-jacket masked in brown
    shop-paper
Lest a passenger peep.

WRITING AT THE WINDOW

May each and every deciduous twist
Of this bonsai verse I am plaiting here
Be worth the terraced conifers
Felled for foolscap in industrial forests.

May that sterile boscage without birdsong
Be redeemed for me by the herring gull
Who feeds from the madwoman's upraised hand
On the next-door neighbours' crazy-paved patio

Where she stands like a Statue of Liberty,
Her lamp a lump of jellied Purina,
Her toga a nightie smudged with a steam-iron.
May my own words dry in the key of dementia.

This isn't Buchenwald, even in German.
This is red-brick, bohemian Beechwood,
Where my WhatsApp group have been texting me
Alerts of *a strange man, sallow skinned,*

Limping along the tidy tram-lines
At the bush forsythia of our back-yard walls.
May my wizened micro-miniature leaves

Be a pruned and potted signage, so,

A shade of sorts in the anticyclone,
A jerry-build in the pelting squall
Of this, our odd lives' beautiful ordeal.
May it mouth a mute allowance for all,

The IVFs in their BMWs
With their power hoses and pest-controls,
And me with my lasered Venetian blindness.
As a ring-tone tape-loop in the church-tower

Bangs out the Bells of the Angelus jingle
I am trimming this try at a dwarf cypress
For my true patron, a pagan of gable-ends,
Who scratched on a plaster wall in Pompeii

A semester before the catastrophe:
Here in this very lane-way, look,
Phoebus the perfume-seller strayed
Five minutes for one glorious fuck.

AISLING AT ORLY

It's the final end and exit of *L'imaginaire*
Irlandais sometime in 1996,
The poets returning to their *secondaires*
To versify crossing the River Styx.

There's air-conditioned, underfloor heating.
The bar in the terminal building hums
To the craic of our sterling Republican puns
As Somalis squat to clean the urinal.

There are no hard borders in our Duty-Free.
All of the Northern cohort, hoarding
Cartons of brandy, claret and fags,
Are shoulder to shoulder beside Yours Truly,

An interloper, a looper from Dublin,
With the limited paperback French edition
Of his minor middle-class karaoke
Plus a couple of scrolled-up top-shelf mags.

None of us is saying anything
As we fish in our pockets for formal identikits:
Photo-fit, true-blue passports for six

And a half-dozen green ones for the ex-Catholics.

But that is a different class of colour-scheme.
Red for anger and yellow for fear
Make a perfect orange, says the poet-in-residence
In a Uni where only the Audis back-fire.

We exchange addresses, who are utterly rootless:
We, the footloose *campusinos*,
The anti-clerics of élite establishments,
The Republic of Letters' Oldest Pretenders.

Desert-boots planted on business-class carpets,
It is take-off time to imaginary Irelands
As we shuffle our psalters in galley-proof pages
On quality paper from well-managed woodlands.

CLIMATE CHANGE

The first smooth hammerhead and a bowhead whale
Torpedo the new, the never-before-seen
Sponge reefs and algae bloom of West Kerry waters.
The dolphin's gone. Wades in an Arctic walrus.
The slipper lobster follows, then a harlequin ladybird,
The little egret too and the orange sallow moth.
Car-washes are cancelled. Barbecues without drizzle
Smoke-signal our shit-hot suburbs to Google Earth.

The last turf-fire, the last use of *do be* and *amn't I*;
The last embarrassed hotel wedding-night;
The last Sister of Mercy, the last Month's Mind in Irish,
And the last Down Syndrome child in all Ireland.

DOING THE STATIONS

On the vintage steam train to the camp at Mosney
I'm dressed as a redcoat in a stovepipe shako,
My daughter in dungarees. Come the third millennium,
She'll inter-rail with her pals to the ramp at Auschwitz.

But for now, at the end-stop of my childhood's century,
The red-caps march us straight to the swimming baths.
We crowd at the window of the underground pool-view
To a parents' vision: the ascension of toddlers.

Fast forward thirty years, on the Belfast *Enterprise*.
It's the umpteenth anniversary of internment
With an Arts Council marathon poetry reading
And the formal opening of the Magdalen museum.

The hostess trolley girl takes sterling or Euro, sir.
There's a glimpse of the narrow-gauge backside of Butlin's
Where the rainbow refugees in direct provision
Are not displaced persons. They are guests of the nation.

I think of my father laying down the railway sleepers
In the sunken garden behind our potting-shed
And the pathway of tram-stones from our glass veranda

To the Latin numerals of the clockwork-golf green.

I think of my daughter mugged for her bum-bag
In the Berlin Hauptbahnhof en route to Skopje,
And I think of my portable Remington typewriter
Left in the luggage rack somewhere in Westphalia.

I like to imagine it has done all the stations since,
Coupling, uncoupling, Salonica, Westerbork, Cork,
Coming closer, coming closer, the hammer-blow of its
    pistons,
To the guards at their singalong outside the sentry-posts.

AT THE ABBEY BAR

Across the street at the fronted homeless shelter,
The door is locked until the last call, ladies and gentlemen.
They gather there on the steps like a Greek theatre,
The girl who slept all day in the National Library
And the man who drinks in spurts from a hand-sanitiser,
His corduroys padded with tabloids against the wind-
    tunnel.
Then the ushers call time curtly. The shelter opens.
Cans are crushed. Stem-glasses drained. The play is
    starting.
The poor pass on inside, and the playgoers settle.

We sit for something prolish and unwholesome,
Middle-class actors self-harming in a squat
With anthropological accuracy in their accents
And a minimalist set that's a miracle of economy.
(There's a man from the Arts Council I need to talk to.)
When the mobile alarm for my meds went off in the
    third act,
I wanted to be with them, watching *Dynasty,*
Or even *The Real Housewives of Beverley Hills.*
In there, my blister-foil's worth its weight in silver.

The gallery doors burst open. It's interval time.
Enormous men froth at the bar. They grade performances
While their women queue for the two toilet cubicles
With a wrapped sanitary pad in their Marc Jacob clutch
    bags.
This, the intermission, is the main show, you see. It is
    lights-up.
And over there, through the two-way barrack windows,
Real frost on plain glass explodes with a soap's strobe-light
As the fox on the fly to Cafolla's along the tram-lines
Savours the slipstream of piss and powder; then exits left.

TRANSLATION FROM THE ORIGINAL
from the Greek of Melissa Bambakouri

I don't want to write victim lyrics
About period dramas on a failed first date
Or even about my post-partum sister
Expressing milk in her off-white wedding dress
Under the tinsel crown the archpriest lifted.

Not kitchen-sink poetry, either – neonates
Rinsed in a stone basin of Fairy Liquid –
Or the wisdom of age-old island women,
Their hands like bread-loaves in their black laps,
Who wait on the quay for German tourists.

That sort of kitsch is for men only,
For my changeling younger brother,
A gob-shite from his two-year term in the army,
Or the silver-surfer poet-in-residence
Groping my arse at a key cocktail party

With its Parthenon view from Kolonaki.
Spare me the prolier-than-thou crew, too,
Light from the left in oleographs of Piraeus
Where houseflies blacken a Vapona strip

Over greasy, water-proof oil cloth with olives.

And the larger picture, politics?
I don't mind Macedonia one blind bit;
Cyprus might as well be Northern Ireland.
And the crash of 2008? Was when I taught Papa,
A stroke victim, to mumble alpha to omega.

We started with old Ladybirds he'd bought me,
Bullet-points in the tabloids, a child's Bible.
If the UTI hadn't finished him, we'd have read
Translations from his box-set of World's Classics,
Ancient Greek to him now in their uncut pages.

BOARDING PASS FOR AN EX-PAT

Where you're headed now, down under,
With a turf-sod wrapped in tinfoil and excess baggage
Is beyond the beyond altogether.

Sure, you can drive to the shops with the top down
But bring home none of the messages,
Rashers, Cheese & Onion, Blue Nun, new potatoes.

Rain on your roof will never be lashing;
You'll be drenched the odd time but not drowned.
There'll be hot-water bottles for that, right enough,

But no nice jar down the bed from here on in.
Live till you're ninety plus, please God,
You won't once have the time on you, or the spondulics,

Or the time difference, the more or minus
An hour, is it, to our Easter midnight vigil
In your April-maybe-May Mí na Marbh winter.

When the medic neighbours come again to dinner
Will you miss the old shower, the shit-heads
You could lose the rag with, head the ball back,

Hit the city, prance the dance-floor, act the maggot
In a mill of your best mates from Belfield Med
On the mitch from the wives' and girlfriends' bitch-craft?

You'll think Bray Head at Bondi. I tell you no lie.
You'll be beached there, stranded without one.
Even the stars you study will be hot gas, stellar masses.

Here, they're only beautiful, the Plough, etc.,
The whole shebang of them. Still, whatever your future,
You can't make a hames of it on the far side.

Sit for the Sunday service; stand for the barbecue:
You won't get a quick twelve Mass where you're landed.
You'll be tired, not jaded, never knackered,

Drunk but never mouldy, not ossified.
If you've a heart in you at all, when it goes and breaks
It won't be in smithereens, won't be astray in you,

Or have you crucified the way some folk I could mention.
Though you're only just after ringing this minute ago
With a deadly bit of audio out the back –

A kookaburra gone mental on the decking –

The chestiness of your breath on the handset
Is the real breeze of Melbourne where you're chilling.

Even when your two-and-a-half kids are crawling in
    Melbun
The worst of it is there's nobody next nor nearest
Will call you by your right name with a fada from now on.

O, you may well tell me on this new texting yoke,
The mobile thingies in the Dart at Glenageary:
Thanks a million, boy, for the ochón, ochón ó.

Don't be talking that way to herself, for Jaysus' sake.
You have me buried already, so you do.
To the which of course: *I have in me hole, you bollocks,*

As the fellow said to the bishop. Excuse my Pass Irish.
It's well you may think we'll all get over it,
The wandering wild goose, so we will. But we won't.

You may think I'm going on and on, giving out yards.
But I amn't. Not at all. Or not really.
What I say is: Fair play to you, so, and no bother.

Not a blind bit, little brother. I'll see you later.

It crossed my mind, today must be yesterday where you are;
Or is it? You were the one with the brains. *Slán* for now.

HIGH TIDINGS

Just as in old Saint Matthew's, deep in Irishtown,
Among the bridged ring-roads and the residential tower-
    blocks,
Where the 1720 aquatint in the vestry shows the church
Soaring on a boulder of bedrock in an ochre cope of kelp
And ringed by fishing boats that have rowed from
    Townsend Street
To the sound of its small ship's bell in becalmed water,

There will be frogmen with flippers and halogen torches
Angling among the pillars of the church where I was
    christened,
Its encrusted stations of the cross, its caryatid saints
Dissolving among the octopus and the abalone.
The archipelago where I coast will be atolls of coral,
And the breadbasket of Ballsbridge a begging bowl.

Lakelands, which raised my mother, will be underwater,
And Sandymount sink like Venice. This morning a broker
Tasted the grass for salt in my brother's back-garden.
My daughters have bought their houses a whole mile higher,
All mud and motte-and-bailey against the outlandish
Enlargement of font as their father's eyesight fails them.

MONDAY AT MASS

Mrs McLaughlin's husky from Alaska
Slouched in the bench beside her as she whispered
Sorrowful decades to her husband's plaque
Misting the space where her own name would be added.

The dog smelled of rugby boots on a radiator
And slurped his drool on the roses in the hassocks.
But when I rang the bell for consecration,
My father said his fur was dark italics

Like a Mohican haircut, and he howled
A moon-howl in the Old Norse of the wolf.
You could see down into his throat as his canines crooned.
The dog knew something Mrs McLaughlin couldn't:

That fish stood still in the river at Donnybrook bridge.
The heron shivered midstream on a bicycle's mudguard,
And the bluebottle shipped its wings on the stained glass-
    window.
Mrs McLaughlin covered her face with posh, pink gloves.

I rang the bell for the blood. Monday was no more Monday.
He was the heart of a happening. He was Good Friday now,

Drum of the tundra's hum in the key of dune.
I thumbed the tongue of the bell and the church breathed
    again.

After the twelve o'clock, at the newspaper stand,
He was all chucks under the chin and tummy-tickles.
Our eyes might have met for a moment in recognition.
I did not stroke him. Nor did he roll over.

THREE NUNS

Sr Ignatius, a Charity chiropodist,
Genuflects at the sight of my swollen foot.
I tell her the Greek term is Oedipus,
And she laughs like the Dalai Lama does.
The large nail of the left foot floats
On the ooze of my August weekend walkabout.
Out the back of the two-up, two-down terrace
A nanny-goat called Beatrice bleats.
She's squeezed a couple of dizzy, drenched kids
Onto bedding-straw in a West Kerry kennel
For a widow and children somewhere in Senegal.

Sr Mary, an Ursuline teacher,
Reads the Remedials *Romeo and Juliet*
As their Inter Cert text in a prefab classroom.
Then the stereo skid of a stolen hot-rod
And the cinema scent of scorched rubber
Brings no tuxedo beau from Verona
But a buzz-cut boy-friend from a brutalist high-rise
Who's stripped the silencer from the Mini's exhaust.
The girl who's a Goth is shot out the window.
A grin. They're gone. And the teacher's in tears.
She tells the third years: 'Isn't that beautiful?'

And Cecilia, a Mercy theatre-sister,
Swabs my father's forehead like a scrub-nurse.
She's been in love since before the War
In the bright lights, among the suture needles,
And the convent cubicle: one bed, one kneeler;
Foghorn and phosphor from the lighthouse lantern.
Half a hundred years later,
We'll meet on the pier as the gale-force gathers.
She'll lean against it like a white italic
And tell me: 'I'll be gone like the wind, pet.
The wind has the last word always. I'll be Scarlett.'

BULLETED

Straplines, helplines, lines drawn in the sand.
There's another American mass killing today,
Another White Paper on race relations and riots;
Another fallen, flat-packed biblical city
Plus the premature death of our President's pet Red Setter.
Later, after the ad-break, leaf-blowers against teargas.
The saline drip of the iceberg. Masks. A meltdown.

Each night the sunset passes with flying colours;
Each morning the day emerges in ashes and embers
That startled me once in their painterly slate and salmon.
Pedestrian streets have emptied like a coup d'état.
In the tall building with the worn mahogany bannisters
Where my wife laboured through a cold-snap snow-storm,
The kitchen is boiling kids in their mother's milk.
Even the sterile are untouchable, even the clean unclean,
In these, the metamorphoses of Covid.

Listen to the taps run, the shower-heads, the hair-dryers.
Manhandled women cling to a chamber orchestra –
Vivaldi's *Seasons* down the on-hold hotline –
And crouch in radio silence in their submarine bathroom.
Hear the bootleg cassette tape – cicadas with clarinet siren –

As the fellow from Rentokil, a Syrian in Ongar,
Hoists his ghetto-blaster near the Neighbourhood Watch
 warning.
At breakfast his unmarked van is parked at my own front
 door.
An aroma of morgue in the padded upstairs hot-press
Has nosed the designer dungarees of my first grand-
 daughter.

The churches too are barred, their stained-glass stories
 redacted.
Can I show her an Order of Service on the far side of the
 cattle-grid,
Behind the parish warning about the tort of trespass,
Some twenty-twenty vision of the Year of the Sword, CE?
There's an entrance hymn of sorts in the futile crocus,
Kyrie of a crushed daffodil, a magnolia tree, maybe,
Whistling a minor Gloria through the slow fast of Lent,
And the fifth gospel in Greek, that of the bluebell patch
Where I lay with her Nana once in another millennium.

Her tongue opened my lips, and I sang her praise –
The shape-shift of her buttocks under muslin
Were the apricots of Anti-Lebanon – not caring
That the Christian militia had sacked the camp at Chatila;

Or that the paper's morning edition had bannered
The black, block-letter headline of *Ceasefire Declared;*
Though the early afternoon run, the *Herald* at noon,
In a stop-press, pink-font newsflash on the back-page
Among the births and bedsit lettings, said *Ceasefire Broken.*

Three months after she entered, white-robed,
The stud-holes in her earlobes closed.

Then the Council came. They would all hear it,
The start on wireless, the end on rabbit ears.

When she stripped away her charcoal habit,
The mother unveiled a silly shy novice;

Yet old men stood on the No. 10 bus-route
For the cancer patient boarding its open-back

In the dark blue suit and the sensible loafers.
Her pet-name died with her daddy's last stroke.

Though nieces called her by her own baptismal
She'd sign off: *Yours in JC, Thomas.*

Aside from the shot at a rebel anthem
She wrote for a troop of Ibo commandoes –

Its chorus *Biafra Once Again!* –
To a tune her Munster grandfather crooned,

And the monsoon month of June in a drained
Hotel pool among young, drugged Muslim

Guards with grenades and rosary beads
Around their necks and their flak jackets,

There is nothing else worth a newspaper notice.
Decades of hopscotch and Astroturf rotas

As Sister Scone of the junior school tuck-shop,
Sacristan of the locked tabernacle

And a tutor lip-reading in the library
With a D-stream Cerebral Palsy pupil.

After the Mater hysterectomy
She asked to inspect her sleeper agent:

*'I was born with all my eggs. Imagine.
The new biology teacher's a genius.'*

But that was the hit from the pethidine drip.
Now her faux-granite, shamrock-shaped plaque –

Two fat ladies in the math of a mass grave –

References a male roll-call of aliases

On a wall-tablet the builders have bulldozed.
Her convent bedroom's a boutique *ensuite*

For lay folk on a breakaway retreat;
A walk-in shower where the *prie dieu* moaned

Under the onus of a brand-new knee-cap
To steady her step as she stooped at last

With large-font missal and silicone femur,
To hand on down what we are handing over.

BAREFOOT BLUES

Late at lunchtime on that last Holy Thursday
I dithered outside the pop-up, new nail parlour –
Shuffling, by way of a kick-off, from one foot to another –
Where the Thai chiropodist smiles and talks gridlock
As she grooms the stub of the toe and wipes away talcum.

The inflammation is as clear as crystals.
I had been perched at home on the edge of the bath
With ointment oozing on the butter-scraper
In the smell of the wife's hand-cream from Jo Malone,
Its odour of almond and olive like the Holy Land.

In the days of the perishing library, the fingerless gloves,
I'd steep my chilblains in a pan of her hot urine
Or bed them beside hers in the cool sediment
Of the shallows of the stream at the site of Olympia
Where the fleet-footed flashed past, according to Pindar.

There were the no-show ankle socks on a wedding-night,
An ice-pack of peas in place of a hot water-bottle,
And the stumps, like an amputee's, where the nails would
    be pulled.
There was the Frankenstein lurch of a footfall

On jokey walkabout with the gunshot acids of gout.

I have been shod, in short. I have been slipshod;
Footloose when it was fashionable, footless when it was not.
They have stood their ground like a brace of Third World
    mules,
While the earth races beneath them at the speed
Of the lines of the crucified poles on the Inter-rail east.

Who told them they were naked and not nude?
Who told them they were thankless proletarians,
Shoehorned in sneakers and sandals like thalidomide fins?
You would need the long-bristled brush of a master,
Made from the Titian hair of the woman who washed

The horrible feet of Jesus with her Oil of Olay
To say: You are fondled too. You are never to be forgotten.
When the sheet in the morgue with its usual lack of
    attention
Lifts and let slip the last step of the journey,
A worn-away rubber-back carpet under a writing desk

Inscribes the only hint of the tongue-tied boots in the
    bonfire.
No-one will find them in the family photograph albums;

The socks are not bequeathed like a snuff-box or an onyx.
When they called me up that night for the foot-washing,
I held out my hands to the priest with the towel to rinse
   them.

MERIDIANS

One yellow with cellotape, the other buoyed in bubble-
    wrap.
Which to make time for, which to keep fast beside me?
The housekeeper's clock, bought from her Green Shield
    stamps,
Or my father's antique stopwatch from Switzerland.

Its face is fogged still from the Dragon races
Each Thursday club-night from May to September.
There's a scent of harbour-mouth on the fob's
Ribbon, no print of his opposable thumb

To trigger the countdown to the starting pistol.
Hers was set for six-thirty. We would all sleep through it
And wake to breakfast and to packed school lunches
With our names initialled on the hard bananas.

The stopwatch works its passage. Ditto the bedside clock.
I wind them both now to unwind them as one. Their
    two ticks
Teem in an undertone that is not synched tinnitus
But seethes with the stillness of their sleep gone astray
    on me.

It is broad moonlight here. It is Covid quiet
With the miracle of no wind in my North Atlantic
    box-room.
The dials from Clery's store and La Chaux de Fonds
Wheeze with the low pneumonia of oars in rowlocks

Amid the chuckle of crickets in pilgrim Pietrelcina,
And both, for a nanosecond, merge from their underground
Like the nymph cicadas in the foliage of olives
To hiss in my ear: siestas, too, are for listening.

BLOOMSDAY

for Peter Sirr

What began as the Solemnity of Corpus Christi
Passionflowers twice as the feast of the fruit of the body.
Same-old; same-new. Flesh and booze of the boulevard.

We start with urinous kidneys at the Martello,
A ringfort built to withstand a French invasion –
That's Joyce the joker for you, communing in Paris –

And end in the muddle of noisy *in medias res*
Where we follow old rooflines and not new storefronts
In our tourist-trail Potemkin polity.

It's bellybuttons and bottoms-up all day;
Boaters and corsetry. Thongs under bustles
And the retro décor scent of the snug near Finn's Hotel

Where we read aloud choice incarnational cuts
Of rump-steak from her stream-of-consciousness come-on.
In a mezzanine named for Molly (Bloom or Malone?)

We know the Polish for *Please*, the Mandarin for *Thank You*,
A Brazilian's bright *De Nada,* but the creole waitress

With the matador's arse and the bow-tie is puzzled by
   Stout.

And out in the midsummer, Mediterranean streets
Among blue plaques, boot-scrapers, and the halogen of
   building sites
An Odyssey of new Dubliners awaits its artisan portrait.

They are queueing there with the patience of Jobstown
   and Ongar
At bus-stops with signage we cannot even pronounce
But which seem to pronounce upon us and the footfall
   of loafers

As we Luas home with leap-cards to the Latin Quarter
He called in *Exiles* a new suburb outside Dublin city:
The red-brick boutique Airbnb of Ranelagh village.

We are neither citizens nor denizens now but the migrant
   ex-pats
Of our own infancy, of our civil mantelpiece memories,
Where a renal nurse from Manila is teaching me Tagalog.

THE SELF AND THE *SELVA*

Like that canto in Dante,
Its famous first tercet
Where he couldn't distinguish
The trees from the forest.

Far enough in a fir-wood,
You'll soon find the stockade
Where chinks in the planking
Still suck like harmonicas.

Or else it's at Christmas
With the shedding, the non-shedding;
White snow on the branch-lines
From an aerosol paint-spray.

Either way, you just kneel there
With the hardened star in your palm
And listen to no phoenix
Fine-tuning from charcoal grit

The might-have-been birdsong
Of the *turdus* Jesus blessed,

Its nest a halo of human hair
In the fig-tree that he cursed.

Holocaust Memorial Day, 2020

IN THE WAKE OF A WEDDING

The Thames the colour of beer, brown froth,
But a dry bar on the boat's reverse cruise,
And the belly dance of a Muslim mother
Surrounding my nephew's Baghdad bride.

There's her granny or a grand aunt there,
Togged out like a Poor Clare nun
Near the Dublin library where I used to borrow
Books about Gordon of Khartoum

Or the boy who stood on the burning deck.
She points in turn to Waterloo Sunset,
To the Tower of London, to Canary Wharf.
That, she tells me, was where you bombed them,

And she recommends the Mary Poppins
Pilgrimage around St Paul's
When all I want would be Brendan Bracken's
Stall in the War Rooms under Whitehall.

We sit in silence as the bridesmaids trill
And scatter paper petals. I have one still,
Pressed in a paperback Koran,

A Greenwich time-keep at Gravesend

With its forty shades of a shot at turquoise.
While we benchmark, elders inhaling each other,
She announces: 'I so admire the Irish.
I gather they always pray *Please God*,

Inshallah, just the same as ourselves.'
So I tell her I've heard Our Lady's Sura
Read at a Christmas Midnight Mass.
Then skiffle and snare drum, strobe lights stop us

And I slip to the stern with an infidel's bootleg.
Light wanes. The couples waltz. The river's all
Dickens and Conrad to the Isle of Dogs.
The whole of my childhood churns in its wake,

Along with Aladdin, the paladin Saladin,
Bin Laden, the hashish of assassins,
And my sign of the cross, a Pavlovian salaam,
When an ambulance siren calls me to prayer.

THE HALLOWEEN PARTY

I hoist a knitted skeleton on a drip-stand in the porch.
The children are coming, a hundred and twenty last year.
Remember the white-face zombie in her communion dress
And the imp with the actual scythe and his separated father
Standing shyly out at the gate as if it were Saturday?
Later, the lights gone out in the scared terraces,
There will be no safe house for the lads in the black
  bin-liners.

I place a candle on the ledge of the lunette to illumine
A later myth than the carnival of Samhain –
This is no shambles, it tells me, *this is Shangri La*;
The Fall, the Flood, those are our fathers' phantoms.
But a bumble-bee with long yellow stockings of pollen
Gorges on a folding passion-flower and cannot help herself
On the eve of November as the month of the dead begins.

PRINCE ALBERT'S LAST STAND

I had to travel south to Sydney, Australia,
To find your missus ruminating glumly,
Arsed on her glutes in an upside-down universe.

But you're still upright in Dublin, albeit behind guard-rails,
With a good head on your frail shoulders
Near the gate to the Natural History Museum

Where I used to bring my three year-old daughter
To breathe on the glass cases of native species
She will never see in her long lifetime,

Just as my father held my pullover sleeve
Up the slippery spiral staircase
To the wire-cage at the top of Nelson's Pillar.

You're painted as a prig, a prim Lutheran,
Yet your bride's journal notes the wedding night
Was 'most gratifying' in a queer cuttlefish flurry.

That squiggle of white bird-shit on your skull
Could be the imagined migraine of one
Blurred humanitarian's iron demurral.

Child labour in the coal-mines, the main thing,
With Gold Coast slavers, libraries' late night hours,
Piped water closets in model cottages;

Then daguerrotypes of the whole world's art-works
In a cheap omnibus volume, plus a bursary
To explore why photographs fade in strong sunlight

But brighten like a smile slowly in darkness,
The way you're hiding there in plain sight of the street
And the lie of the land like a Palmyra column.

After the fuss over the Shelbourne Nubians,
It can't be long now. Stand on your own clay feet
And keep the head down, Albert. There's a good man.

III

*I speak to the living as if they were dead
and to the dead as if they were living.*

—Diderot

CATECHESIS OF THE POET AND THE POEM

Who?
A blind woman with a file of sighted children.
The lines she draws like days onto blank wallpaper
Are the watermarks of their height as measured in hands
After the Fall, of course, and before the Flood's harvest.

What?
It is like a drop-leaf hunting-table that is perfectly laid,
With white linen cloth lit by a ship's decanter
At which all the prayers of the prey of the world and
    his wife
Sit to savour on China plate their own *ichthus* and chips.

When?
In the silence of the last Waterloo flush of your fellow man,
While waiting through the wind-down of his warm-air
    hand dryer
And the strict latch in the lockset of the toilet entrance
    slammed
For the whole weight of the world to pass from you finally.

How?
In a rumour spread from mouth to mouth like a herpes,

In the sorbet of sharp vodka on a tongue's tiny paper-cut;
In the gell of the ooze from a piercing stud in a lobe
That is worth the wait for the drip of its gold drop-earring.

Where?
In the hermitage behind stairs in any termitary;
In the priest's hole of a yard in a bedsit semi
Where the rain has turned the sandstone to terracotta
And a sprig of wet mint sways on its own fossil.

Why?
To parcel Van Gogh's ear in a registered envelope
To every poor Beethoven straining at a Third
And have them score their trumpeted Napoleons
For the pizzicato of spoon and bones and of washboard.

WIND IN THE CHIMNEY

Moved home to an old house
And a bare back-room in 2000,

There's no call for that sound now
From the BBC SFX catalogue.

Its moan is stored on my mobile:
An acoustic for monologues,

A boom ghosting the outside
World of the close neighbourhood,

The hue and cry, the hullabaloo.
There's a roped bamboo pan flute

In the low notes of the swallow,
In a rock-pigeon's cooing down the cold

Terracotta pot that is smokeless,
And the thin whine of the uileann pipes

If the breeze seethes in the linden;
Then the didgeridoo of the Honda's

Home-delivery ponies.
Shofar horn of the ordinary,

Your soot-fall of feathers and moss twigs
Favoured me once with a shoe-lace

From some rogue magpie's swag.
Grandest of all in the fire grate, though,

Was the prized pearl of a hailstone. So
From the sheet-music of my pine shelves,

Chamber of my listening flue,
I scoop spit from its saxophone bowl

For my own audition at woodwind:
The hum of a mouth-harp's solo blues.

CLEARINGS

La chair est triste, hélas! et j'ai lu tous les livres – Mallarmé

In the time that it's taken Yours Truly
To hew and chuck a couple of skewed quatrains,
My neighbour's amputated tree
Has turned into corporate statuary

For some City accountant's atrium
That was once, at supper, my five-o'clock shadow,
At breakfast, a fir-tree in a fountain of mint.
Yet, when the tree-surgeon waves at my window,

I wave straight back at him. We're sodality men,
And this is no eco-friendly pastoral.
He has logged all day. I am logging in now,
My humming printer's renewable forest

White-water rafting down River Rapid
The cedar and redwood of biblical lives
To pulp into chipboard, into yellow-pack poems
For the poetry editor's log-jammed backlog

Where they're planted between the rental villa
In Tuscany and the risqué sketch, always

Within Scopes 1, 2, 3, of its carbon emissions
As defined by the Greenhouse Gas Commission.

A CIRCULAR LETTER

In the commodious bedpan of Dublin Bay
If you throw yourself from the pier at Dun Laoghaire
The tide will flush you to the dunes of Bull Island.

Thus, one who abandoned paperbacks on the bus,
The 46A, like a mad mobile librarian,
For another mystery to parse in the seat over the engine.

Ditto the voiceover artist with Titian hair
Whose silences linger among the lines like the thumb-
    smudge
On Richard Burton's reading of *Under Milkwood*.

I walked each one of them, harbour and mucky strand,
In the Brylcreem slipstream of my father's trilby.
He talked about links and courses and the common lizard,

Of Captain Bligh and the strand's seaward sandbar
Rising like the Red Sea sediments out of white water,
A land unfolding in foam. In the Beaufort breeze

Of a force-five gale my mouth was a saline windsock,
Speechless, bespoke, with mercury dental amalgam,

And a Faber hardback at home bookmarked with bus-
    tickets.

Forgive us our deaths, O Lord. Forgive us our dying too,
As we forgive you for having created us first
With the words of the song of the sea tattooed on the skin
    of our teeth.

I was playing with my infant daughters on the East Pier
    bandstand
Near the queue at the Whippy van, when the old man
    floated past,
That last time in the summer of Princess Di; and I waved
    to him.

He tilted his trilby, and smiled, and went on; and was lost,
Guiding my mother's ocelot coat, in the Sunday sea of the
    shore-dwellers.
Though my adult children remember it differently:

How there were swings and roundabouts down at the
    lighthouse,
And how the big wind lifted the brim of my straw boater
And flung it into the air where a gust from the West
    far-fetched it –

I can hear the girl on the bus say, *'There's no apostrophe missing'*
And the actor's greenroom recital, *'A way a lone a last'*–
Among mackerel fishing lines and the weight of lead sinkers.

PAN PIPE

The drowned sheep in the sand
Drowsed like an Elgin marble.
Going inland, we could hear
Caterpillars nibble dark foliage.

On the far cliff of the island
Near the egg-white monastery wall
The red-bearded elder
Bawled *Bobby Sands good,*

Margaret Thatcher bad,
A salute from his cell-door
With ouzo and almond nougat.
When he rumpled your headscarf

The trinket medals tinkled
Like the goat-bell that guided us
One rolled cigarette away
To the slab of a washing stone.

In the room underneath us
They had laid out an old man
And hung a Vapona strip

Like a sanitary pad from a light-bulb.

That night your centre-parting
Where the roots glowed titian
Strayed like a rabbit run
Through brushwood, marram grass,

The headless statues of heroes,
Gold-leaf icon of dusk
And the lizard stunned on a pedestal,
To break at last on the right beach.

MAKING WAVES
for Kevin Brew

I have left the control-room and the studio sound-desk
For the dead acoustic of my own live labyrinth,
A sonar of souterrains, potholes and catacombs,
And the low, leather-bound static of pipistrelles
Hung upside down in the dark like old headphones.

Listen here as the pygmy women of the Cameroons
Pound the river's vinyl with the white flat of their palms,
Drumming the dawn awake. That's the *tambour d'eau;*
And this, the mouth-music of those Arctic Aleuts
Whose only narcotic is the drone of deep breathing.

Now to the prayer-call of the mud mosque in Mali
Or the Maronite deaconesses of Mount Lebanon
With the sharp acrylic glitter of their contralto.
Then the bold-as-brass concerto of Athens traffic
Heard in the lobe of the blind-as-a-bat boot-black

At the underground portal in Omonia Square.
Now give me the bubbled gulp of a wooden
Hull in the swell which is clinkered and not fibreglass.
That sunlit city classroom in the summer recess

Will have no seagulls' doggerel over the schoolyard.

Eavesdrop, so, like the oculus in the monstrance
Of the Blessed Sacrament chapel in D'Olier Street:
The pneumatic brakes of a bus, yes, drizzle on hoodies,
To frame the irregular footfall, an auricle stopping
To step over a sleeping-bag in the wet atrium.

NO HEAD FOR HEIGHTS

The seashells at the summit
Of deep Mount Everest mark
The wreck of the real Ark,
And its animals, two by two,
A male with American teeth
And the frozen smile on a Sherpa.

Below, back at base-camp,
Wags watch through lorgnettes
As queues peak in the Death Zone
At a cryogenic chevron
Of corpses nobody escalates.
But the cappuccino cloud-shapes

Shape-shift beneath the climbers
To cover the gridlocked glacier
Like a nebula seen from the Gods.
They are texting sweethearts selfies
Of goggles and oxygen masks
As they squat on a breathless seabed

Where the stumbling block of stones,
Miles from its first flood tide,

Is a shofar of ammonite fossils.
Back at base-camp, on dry land,
It is pigeons that peck at ring-pulls
And the blister packs of vitamins;

While the Nepalese babbler bird,
Whose bloodline is pure T-Rex,
Makes do with the foam of snow-storms
That can never fashion a rainbow,
And the altitude sickness of those
Who tiptoe down here on the topsoil.

SHIBUI

The Sacred Heart sister at Sophia
Posts me an airmail letter
With two sought-after stamps
For her twelve year-old collector.

Much later, on cassette,
She talks of doing a doctorate
On etiquette in Edo,
Plus a traveller's guide for the Gaijin.

The millennium hosts its moment;
A tsunami coasts toward Christmas.
She tells me on the telephone
Of an essay on Shusako Endo,

The convert Catholic novelist,
His link an east-west ligature
And a job for her jubilee year.
Call and response continue

From the '64 Olympics
To the karaoke bar
She runs with an Irish Jesuit

For mystical male alcoholics.

She has left stone fields in Ireland
For moss in a stone garden,
And the Celtic cross of her convent
For gravel curated in circles.

Now her cancer of the pancreas
Is assigned a last text-message
In the three moonlit lines
Of a Meiji death haiku.

AGAINST THE GRAIN

The quest for the Holy Grail
As Python knew, is a mug's game
For Hollywood heads, high liturgists
And the underage ordained
In bespoke cassock and stock.
Chalice the Greek for *cuppa*,
Cuppa the Latin for tun,
And cup the English for chalice
Or one breast in a bra,
A mouth rooting for milk;
Which is how it all began
For the faithful and the infidel,
For topers and teetotallers,
And the thirst of the ne'er-do-well
With the host glued to their palate.
Earthenware ewer and platter.

Not to mention *poterion*
Or its Aramaic original
Wetting his lips as he sipped
From an unglazed pottery bowl
And passed on hard fingertips
To a few friends in the foetal

Pose on no Persian carpet
But a sheep's-wool Bedouin mat
Grey from a wooden ground-loom;
Which is how it all descended
To the dry and the dehydrated,
To my grandchild with her beaker
As the breadline at Communion
Mulls the radiant ruby wine
And the tipsy, twin-set coeliac.
Earthenware ewer and platter.

CROSSINGS

That night of the gale on the wildcat lake of Galilee,
Jesus, for Christ's sake, drowsed. He dozed
On a futon and a bolster in the fo'c'stle;
Sunk in the sleep of the just, in the red
Rush of his hillside homily, there he was
Wallowing. Waves, the yellow of vomit,
Heaved at the gunwale. The hull threw up.
Mark he wouldn't awaken though they pummelled,
The able-bodied disabled, the disciples.
Then the storm stilled. The waterline lay level.
They had not yet wept together in the same vessel.
Thus the man of might and the men of maybe.

Night of the geckoes in Gethsemane orchard,
Christ, for the sake of Jesus, an insomniac,
Clung to the ground, his nails like a cliff-hanger.
Grave with the terror of lifting into the skyline,
Far from the scent of lilac, the stench of night-soil,
He grasped, and, in the grasping, stood his ground,
He for whom wind-socks served as a sheet-anchor.
His friends were fast asleep. Their breath was winey.
Splayed in the foetal, the beloved ones
Mooned with their mouths wide open, their eye-lids
    battened,

And slept a distance in their terraced sub-plot
From the man of maybe to the men of might.

The smoker's alcove lay in the hotel library.
That's how long ago now. At the vast bay window
I sat in a menstrual smell from the estuary,
Tobacco smoke of cheroots, and the must
Of might-have-been hard-back books behind glass.

What does a poet write? He writes non-fiction.
So here's the thing: *Doomsday* in twelve volumes
By Sir William Alexander, Earl of Stirling,
Anno Domini 1614. Shakespeare was proofing
Tempest and *Winter's Tale* between bad kidney-stones.

You can see the silverfish self-flagellate
Like sperm in their folded paper dormitories.
Now you know, old boy. You, who started with Puffins,
Penguins and Pelicans, can wax-polish away
The two brass wings of the big eagle lectern

With a wet wadding pad until Judgment Day
But you're still spread-eagled on the tarmacadam
Making snow-angels with your shot at green sleeves;
Yet answerable even now to the semi-colon
And the images each dawn panhandles you.

Where was my Ventolin? All those hexameters
Foaming at the mouth made do with doldrums,
Death, and the dream of my own small-hours insomnia:
To compose, to be collected, to be selected. Yes,
I scattered my ashes there in the hotel library.

MARKING TIME

The sower rising and the seed descending,
The strong arm and the broadcast: None of them.
I was the ground of other footfalls, windfalls,
Muck trodden down to a film of alluvium.

My name was mud. My feet and hands were clay.
In the stone basin of the safe-house/madhouse
Pits from a pomegranate choked the sinkhole
While threads of semen trailed in the toilet-bowl.

Came the lazy-acre decade. A languish strangled
The parachute sperm of a huge broadleaf tree
In a maze of milk thistle and chickweed,
Dwarf shrubs where the spittle spiders foamed.

Olive-green tufts sprouted among sandstone,
Tzitzits where I poured in pesticide,
Preferring the rare prints of fossil petals
To the crayon numerals of a child's hopscotch.

The text talks about topsoil. That too is true.
The wild flower of our walled Ranelagh red-brick
Flashed turquoise from its crevice near the gutter,
But the niche, too high for any hose-pipe,

Shrivelled over abortive Irish barbecues.
Even the snowdrops at the scraper failed their feast days
Each Little Christmas. Debris from fire-logs
Blackened the beds manure would have fattened,

Like my grandmother at the horse-trams with a skillet
To fuel her prize-winning coral rhododendrons.
Till, one day, out of the blue, the clear sky, gorgeous
Ordinary, lets drift the rain of God,

Softest of showers, a sprinkling. You stand inside it,
Not kneeling in the kindness of the drizzle,
In the ease and eyewash of just looking up.
Behind the wheelie bin, wet jasmine reeks,

Like the scent of a new book open, breathed in,
A petticoat slipstream at the metal wicket
Where blue tits zigzag to their roasted rice-grains.
There'll be husks, kernels of all kinds to follow,

And today let's start with the stone of an apricot,
With garlic skins and egg-shells in the compost,
For what, you say? For next year's lavender bush
Like the one I watered at the out-patient's entrance.

There'll be a toddler someday on the patio,
Agog at the ants and the underarm hair of scutch.
My hands could be full of hundreds and thousands too,
Strewn freestyle to top a poppy-seed cupcake.

THE ART OF DYING
i.m John Moriarty

It is three days before. It is not the third day after.
You're perched on a stick in a sun-trap on your patio,
And peeling from your head in soft brushstrokes
    of breeze
The last capillaries of all that chemo.

What was once the grey mane of a breaking wave
Is a strand of sinkhole hair in a sandstone yard.
That Aran gansey you're wearing is still scorched
From the time you waved in the ward, and yanked out
    the cannula.

Then a sparrow sits on your shoe-lace, a bright by-passer.
She is sifting a long wisp of the thatch that's thinned
To patch the wicker-work crib of her next nest somewhere
With spit-balls of your lambs-wool waterfall braid.

She has come straight from Lesbia's love-bitten breasts
And the gospel according to Hamlet, the hovering one,
Via a soiled sandal-strap in Nazareth that she lit upon
Long enough to feather a single quivering thought.

And she has cruised through the daze of Bede's sweet
    mead-hall,
Its wood-smoke, weaponry, and the groping of stunned
    girls,
From the sad adobe hole in the far wall of the barn
To no eternal lantern at the last, but the windsock

Of another blind oculus. Now she is passing over
Your dear, deciduous head within a hairsbreadth of it,
A heartfelt loop-of-the-loop till you tear a tuft to throw her,
A tousled kiss-curl lost in the thermal uplift.

YAHWEH AND THE YAHOO

Sweetheart, Saviour, etc., show me today
The yesterday I missed, a kingfisher flash
While I huffed and puffed on my tortoise-shell glasses.

Hatch me a dove and serpent from my breakfast egg.
Send me out among the folk of the three Sabbaths
And the second day of the week for its Monday feeling.

Give us milk and honey without the shit and the bee-stings.
Accept us as we are who pee in the bath
But cannot piss in the shower. Let the middle ground

Of our bodies never be marginalized.
Let me search both high and low for a broad church
With candle-grease on my desert boots from the Vigil.

Do not allow me to long for things I am mortgaged to,
But belong to my losses. Save me from tricksters, pet,
From atrocity chic and the boutique victim lyric.

Let me end this day of fast and feast with no Examen
But an Amen only, or an audible Alleluia.
Let me swallow my psycho-actives with Prosecco

Under the protection of poor Padre Pio,
The patron saint of our ordinary self-harming.
Let me smell my sleeping wife the way I like to,

The West of Ireland scent of her flesh made words
Like the straw of the Brigid's cross a Traveller wove for me
Outside the pharmacy when I was filling my meds.

ON A WING AND A PRAYER

I woke as a child to a frosted window weeping
And the water bottle lukewarm as a wineskin.
I had slept on the edge of the bed for a whole year long
To leave more room for my guardian angel.

It was never a matter of pillow-talk, touch,
Or a prayer for my small big sister in Limbo,
But a brisk napkin roll to the side of the blanket
For the white folds of her laundry-board feathers.

I laid and mislaid her. I moved to dead centre,
To the guards in the barracks, to the angelic *Guardian*,
And the oligarch's gargoyle, a surveillance camera
On a wrapped rooftop for the tradesmen's entrance.

Sleep spoons with me now, mute messenger girl,
On this, my last mattress, a mortuary chapel.
Bring hash for the mother, an eye-drop of breastmilk
To the *amadán* sulking outside of the silo

And the shepherds, too, swaddled in contraband woollens.
Show the saffron monks as they genuflect, grinning,
To their white-headed foetus, a new Dalai Lama,

Who has brought them, barefoot over the ice-floes,

To a yak in its straw shelter, to three
Toy German soldiers of mine, a star in a snow-globe,
And the blonde Madonna with her blue bedfellow's
Frog-legs hobbled in his first station of colic.

VOLI ME TANGERE

Another bore me, another will bury my body.
It's in the Bible or the Greek Anthology.
Either's enough to be going out with.

Meanwhile, I will stand over my life
Though I don't, for the death of me, understand it,
The whole ménagerie of I, me, and my selves.

More of a mud-lark than a muckraker,
Less of a blabbermouth than a glass-blower,
I gulp at the chalice the coeliac hands me

And light my candle off a stranger's intention.
I can piss hard debris down the toilet-bowl
From a blood-brother in the very same shit

And absorb the warmth of a vacant bar-stool
Left by the woman in Human Resources
Whose stem-glass prints a circle on the counter.

I touch and I am touched, digital/manual.
When I arm-wrestled at work with the paraplegic,
I could read the palm of my hand for the first time

As the strongest wrist on the planet shook my fist,
Flush with the mouse and the caked keyboard bar,
Into four fingers and one opposable thumb.

The smell of his hand-sanitizer sank into mine.
I had almost forgotten whose red mobile number
Smeared my small knuckles like a blur of lippy.

Would you perhaps have thought that I was praying
In a mime of the Muslim face-wash, the *wudhu*?
But I was asking my untouchable God

To press pause, then delete, on the glorified body,
And give us instead the mess of the flesh that crawls,
Sweat-pore by sweat-pore, our proper diaspora.

THE LAST ASSIGNMENT

Hopkins was never happier
Than when he lay in the foetal, treading the terrible
    sonnets,
Or Shakespeare, playing a translucent blinder –
Tragic quadruplets in the so-called dark period.

I count my major blessings. They swarm and surface.
When was that moment on the glass-bottom boat tour,
Water as clear as wine at the leper colony
Near Agios Nikolaos, where we swam with snorkels?

I took my troubles then with a pinch of lithium,
Pills in a polished chalice. But these days poems
Pull at my sleeve like smelly toddlers. I lift and let them
Suck at the knuckle of my keystroke fag-end finger.

Two grand-daughters on the terrace stamp in a paddle-pool
And the brand-new Roman blinds in here scroll down
To chaperone a costly oil's impasto
From the patio light of my last Indian summer.

My children are well, thank God. My children are working.
The transplant has stopped hurting. Here I am, Lord.

Look down on me, a developer's drone with camera
Roaming for green-sites where there were bedsits only.

God of Abraham, God of Isaac, God of Aidan, too,
Is this Potemkin village the Paradise Inn
From which at last whole-heartedly to journal
Those years of my life that were April in Chernobyl?

Can I move among the mutants and name them now?
Are my lips still stitched with pink thread like the woman
Whose grimace the mortician couldn't straighten?
Can I letterbox my house-keys like the advocate

Who walked into the sea in a pin-stripe suit?
I think of Hopkins striding through Donnybrook
To read an early Mass for the Mountainville nuns,
Then sharing the final draft over his eggs and bacon,

His face lit up, elated, in the marvelling parlour;
And of Shakespeare, glad and goose-pimpled with pleasure
As a long-ago glacier calves, in a whoosh of whiteness,
Its ghastly, ghost-written word.

WATER UNDER THE BRIDGE

On Donnybrook bridge one day my daughter asked me
Whatever happened to the Kodak moments
Of the Instamatic and our old Polaroid camera?
She was texting a pal the pixels of a vixen
Watching a heron watching a river meander
And adding a pinch of salt to its slow downfall.

The day of the wind that blew my Dad's fedora
Into the Dodder at the new Donnybrook lights
I asked him what had happened to the hats,
The trilbies and the homburgs, the cloth caps
Thrown in the air at the Great War's starting pistol
By bareheaded chaps who would strap on colander helmets.

The No.10 still stopped at Donnybrook bridge,
The time he had asked the same of his own father.
Would a trace of the brass tackle and bridle leather
Or the broad band of the stable's Dutch horse collar
Outlast these tram tracks? He would live to laugh at
Canopied hybrid coupés clamped outside mews.

In the glow of the carriage lamps that had once lit landaus
His great grandchildren pedal a cycle path

Where his cortege paused on the Donnybrook dual
    carriageway.
The papers that morning were full of Sarajevo
And a pontoon made out of roped telegraph poles
For an arch that was under water in warzone Mostar.

But this isn't Heraclitus or his smartass student.
Everything goes and everything goes on.
When the river flooded my grandmother's kitchen
It smelled like the Venice of her golden wedding
As much as any morgue; and when her hunchbacked
    husband
Lifted his bride of half a hundred years

Over the children's pool of the hotel reception
He was saying we build on sand and not on stone.
So, however long it takes, I want them to live –
Away from ponds, of course, and close to clear water –
These toddlers, full of eggs, where my own surname ends
In a punt on a trailer bike across Donnybrook bridge.

PURE FILTH

Metaphysics took my mind off things.
Now I'm coming to my senses,
An astronaut with his head in a washing machine.

I stink, therefore I am. It's a good start.
The pure is sterile; the sterile is unclean.
The stepwell smells like a swimmer's towelling.

That Euro coin's a consecrated host.
It has travelled from bum-bags through tollgates
To a church with a pay-view Tintoretto.

The tongue I clean with an old silver spoon
Has tasted soda bread, the salt of lithium,
And the roll-on deodorant of a suicide.

I take off my glasses to see the blur better
With Vaseline on the lens, muslin from Mosul.
That Hindu airport cleaner clears to a gondolier.

The heart hears. It beats one billion times
For the vole, for the dolphin, for the Down Syndrome,
The Bishops of Rome. Then it listens. Hush.

That was the sane, the insanitary place
Where we bowed down low before the depths we rise to.
Like poor Napoleon to his Josephine,

A creole with her stump of mercury soap,
I call to the world of my own five sensei:
Dearest, I shall be with you tonight. Do not wash.

FILIOQUE

Like Dolmens round my childhood the Northern poets.
At Carrowmore with Montague that time
Among the megaliths with his small, stapled chapbook;
The whine of the wind no blare of Bronze Age horns
But the tintinnabulation of Belfast bin-lids.

Or Heaney reading from *North* in Theatre M
When the college porter ran like a Greek messenger
Down the raked and smoking terraces to tell us
Of a Trojan war-horse stampeding through Dublin
And a volunteer plasma rush to Pelican House.

James Simmons rowed me to an island on Lough Gill
One summer school in Sligo, singing
'The Three Pornographers' in the perfect acoustic
Of windless water. The children of Magda Goebbels
Rose like the dead in the form of the Von Trapp family.

And Mahon slicing a scone in the Shelbourne lounge,
Steward of night-soil and starlight in the dormitory town,
With the one word – *Speak* – on his landline message minder:
The last note 'I am dwindling' from a planetary red dwarf
Who had written the *Miserere* on Mozart's shirt-cuff.

Now those star-chambers of childhood are Northern lights,
And all that remains is the lichen and spider silk
Of the nests of the long-tailed tits of Michael Longley
In the autumn flight of their great Eastern migration
Over the blood-lands, over the bog-lands, over the killing
grounds

To Chekhov's monastery on Sakhalin Island.
There, even a fax from Sandymount fades like a stone-
marker
While our traffic of texts from beneath their borderline
Persists among board-game place-names – Irkutsk,
Kamchatka –
In the storage silos of menthol breath on the iCloud.